Polar Lands

KINGFISHER

a Houghton Mifflin Company imprint
222 Berkeley Street
Boston, Massachusetts 02116
www.houghtonmifflinbooks.com

First published in 2005
2 4 6 8 10 9 7 5 3 1

1TR/0505/PROSP/RNB/140MA/F

LIBRARY OF CONGRESS CATALOGING-IN-PUBLICATION DATA
Hynes, Margaret, 1970-
Polar lands/Margaret Hynes.—1st ed.
p. cm.—(Kingfisher young knowledge)
Includes index.
1. Polar regions—Juvenile literature. I. Title. II. Series.
G590.H96 2005
998—dc22
2004028261

ISBN 0-7534-5868-3
ISBN 978-07534-5868-6

Printed in China

Senior editor: Catherine Brereton
Coordinating editor: Stephanie Pliakas
Designer: Joanne Brown
Cover designer: Poppy Jenkins
Illustrators: Julian Baker, Lee Gibbons
Picture manager: Cee Weston-Baker
DTP manager: Nicky Studdart
DTP operator: Primrose Burton
Artwork archivist: Wendy Allison
Production controller: Jessamy Oldfield
Indexer: Sheila Clewley

Acknowledgments
The publishers would like to thank the following for permission to reproduce their material. Every care has been taken
to trace copyright holders. However, if there have been unintentional omissions or failure to trace copyright holders,
we apologize and will, if informed, endeavor to make corrections in any future edition.
b = bottom, c = center, l = left, t = top, r = right

Cover: Getty Imagebank; 1 Getty Lonely Planet Images; 2–3 Getty Robert Harding Pictures; 4–5 Science Photo Library (SPL)/Doug Allan;
6–7 Getty Taxi; 8–9 Corbis/Tom Bean; 8 SPL/Ted Kinsman; 9 Corbis Ralph A. Clevenger; 10–11 Corbis/Rob Howard; 11tr Getty NGS;
11br Corbis/Darrell Gulin; 12–13 Darrell Gulin; 13tr SPL/Simon Fraser; 13b Corbis/Charles Mauzy; 14–15 Corbis/Dan Guravich; 14b
Oxford Scientific Films/Doug Allan; 15tr Corbis/Kennan Ward; 15cr Nature Picture Library/Tom Vezo; 16–17 B&C Alexander/Arctic Photos;
17br Corbis/Paul A. Souders; 18 Getty Imagebank; 19tl B&C Alexander/Arctic Photos; 19br Nature Picture Library/David Pike; 21t Corbis/Tim
Davis; 21c Natural History Picture Agency/Laurie Campbell, Seapics, Hawaii; 24–25 B&C Alexander/Arctic Photos; 24b Getty Stone;
25b Nature Picture Library/Doc White; 26t Corbis W. Perry Conway; 26b Corbis/Dennis Johnson, Papilio; 27 B&C Alexander/Arctic Photos;
28 B&C Alexander/Arctic Photos; 29tr SPL/Doug Allan; 29bl Ardea/Edwin Mickleburgh; 30–31 B&C Alexander/Arctic Photos;
31t Corbis/Galen Rowell; 32 B&C Alexander/Arctic Photos; 33tl B&C Alexander/Arctic Photos; 33b B&C Alexander/Arctic Photos;
34 B&C Alexander/Arctic Photos; 35t B&C Alexander/Arctic Photos; 35 Alamy/Popperfoto; 36 Alamy/B&C Alexander; 37tl B&C Alexander/
Arctic Photos; 37–38 B&C Alexander/Arctic Photos; 38–39 B&C Alexander/Arctic Photos; 39tl SPL/David Vaughan; 39b B&C Alexander/
Arctic Photos; 40–41 Corbis/Dan Guravich; 41t Corbis/Wolfgang Kaehler; 41 Corbis/Tom Brakefield; 48 B&C Alexander/Arctic Photos

Commissioned photography on pages 42–47 by Andy Crawford.
Thank you to models Harrison Nagle, Joley Theodoulou, and Hayley Sapsford.

KFYK Kingfisher Young Knowledge

Polar Lands

Margaret Hynes

KINGFISHER
BOSTON

Contents

Ends of Earth

North Pole

South Pole

The polar lands are found at the opposite ends of the world, in the far north and south, around the poles. They are the coldest and windiest places on Earth.

Frozen landscape

It is so cold in the polar regions that the land and sea stay frozen for most of the year. Polar animals need to be very tough in order to survive in these conditions.

Adélie penguins

poles—*the points farthest north and farthest south on Earth*

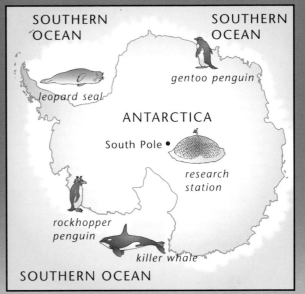

Arctic

The Arctic surrounds the North Pole. It is made up of the Arctic Ocean and the treeless lands around it—called the tundra.

Antarctic

The Antarctic surrounds the South Pole. It is made up of a continent called Antarctica and the Southern Ocean around it.

continent—one of Earth's seven huge areas of land

Frozen features

It is so cold in the polar lands in the winter that snow does not melt. Instead it is pressed into ice as more snow falls on top of it. The ice forms thick sheets that cover the land.

Snowflakes

If you look closely at snowflakes, you will see that they have many different patterns. Almost all snowflakes have six sides (points).

melt—to change from snow or ice into water

Underwater giants

Icebergs are huge chunks of freshwater ice that float in the polar seas. The biggest part of an iceberg lies below the surface of the water.

Crashing ice

Icebergs break off the edges of polar ice sheets and crash into the sea. This mostly happens during the summer when the ice melts a little bit.

freshwater—water that is fresh, like rain or river water, not salty like seawater

Light and dark

The polar lands are unique places. During the long, harsh winters it is dark for almost all day long. In the summer the Sun does not set for many weeks.

Lighting the way

In the summer the Sun dips lower in the sky at night, but it still lights up the land. Even though it is past midnight, these people can find their way home.

unique—not like any other

Strange lights

Near the poles the night skies are sometimes filled with glorious light shows. These spectacular natural displays are called auroras, or the northern and southern lights.

Summer squirreling

The ground squirrel survives the winter by hibernating. In the summer it makes the most of the constant daylight in order to gather a supply of food for the next winter.

hibernating—spending the whole winter in a deep sleep

Tundra in bloom

The tundra is a cold plain that is covered with snow in the winter. When the snow melts in the summer, the tundra comes alive with flowers and animals.

Flowering carpet

A carpet of grasses, mosses, and lichens covers the tundra in the summer. These plants grow close to the ground, escaping the freezing winds that howl above them.

plain—*flat, mainly treeless area of land*

Making seeds in the Sun

In the short summer tundra flowers, such as this Arctic poppy, quickly blossom and produce seeds. Then the seeds stay frozen in the soil all winter long.

Dining alone

Lone grizzly bears roam the tundra when it is in bloom. They feed on mammals, insects, and plants, getting as fat as possible before the winter, when they hibernate in a den.

blossom—to produce flowers

Adaptable animals

Animals that spend the winter in polar lands are specially adapted to survive in freezing temperatures. Many also have white coats so that they cannot be spotted in the snowy landscape.

Antifreeze

This Antarctic ice fish survives in waters where most other fish would freeze solid. It has special chemicals in its body that stop it from freezing.

camouflage—a shape, color, or pattern that helps hide an animal

Changing feathers

In the winter the ptarmigan grows thick white feathers for extra warmth and camouflage in the snow. In the spring it turns brown.

ptarmigan—winter

ptarmigan—spring and summer

Survival of the fattest

There is no danger of this walrus getting cold. Like all sea mammals, it has a thick layer of blubber under its skin. This body fat keeps it warm.

mammals—*warm-blooded animals that feed their young on milk*

Who eats what?

Like all animals, Arctic animals stay busy finding food. Some eat plants, while others are predators. Most animals need to protect themselves from predators.

Protective parents

Musk oxen do not run away when Arctic wolves come close. Instead the adults form a circle around their young so that the wolves cannot catch them.

predators—animals that hunt and eat other animals

Arctic food chain

Arctic wolves are the top predators in this food chain. They eat musk oxen, hares, and lemmings, which feed on grasses and lichens.

eats  *eats*

Arctic wolf

musk ox   *Arctic hare*   *lemming*

eats *eats*

grasses and lichens

Bully bird

In Antarctica the skua is an aggressive predator. It threatens penguins and steals their eggs.

food chain—a diagram that shows who eats what in a specific place

King of the ice

The polar bear is the largest and most powerful hunter in the Arctic. Bears roam alone over long distances each day in search of seals to eat. They also catch fish with their sharp claws.

Surviving the cold

Polar bears spend most of their time on ice floes. They are also excellent swimmers and can spend many hours in the freezing water. Oily fur and a layer of blubber keep these bears warm.

roam—to wander over a large area

Junk food

Polar bears sometimes stray into towns to find food. They also visit garbage dumps, where they may be poisoned or injured.

Mother care

Baby polar bears are called cubs. They are born in a warm, cozy den that their mother digs in the snow. They grow quickly by drinking their mother's rich, fatty milk.

ice floes—*large chunks of floating ice*

Long-distance travel

For many polar birds and mammals, the winter in the Arctic is just too cold. These animals migrate south to warmer places and return again in the spring.

Nomads of the north

Caribou are a type of deer. In the winter they live in forests on the edge of the Arctic. In the summer they travel more than 600 miles north to spend the summer feeding on tundra plants.

migrate—to make the same journey every year at the same time

Flying visits

Arctic terns fly farther than any other birds. Every year they fly from the Arctic to the Antarctic and back, experiencing summer at both poles.

Hardy hooves

Caribou can walk on deep snow without sinking. This is because their wide, fur-fringed hooves act like snowshoes by spreading their weight evenly.

snowshoes—shoes for walking on snow, with frames that are strapped to the feet

Life in polar seas

Polar seas are cold but not as cold and tough to live in as polar lands. The deep waters of the polar seas are teeming with sea creatures.

Antarctic seafloor

Colorful sea anemones, fan worms, and starfish live on the Antarctic seabed. Sea slaters and sea spiders creep along the floor.

a school of fish

sea anemone

sea slater

***teeming**—full of living creatures*

Sea food

Many animals in polar seas, from tiny fish to large whales, feed on plankton. These are microscopic animals and plants that drift in the water.

fan worm

sea spiders
(red and
yellow)

starfish

microscopic—*much too small to be seen with the human eye*

Sea mammals

The polar seas are home to whales, seals, sea lions, and walrus. These mammals have blubber to keep them warm, as well as streamlined bodies that help them move through the water easily.

Making a splash

Whales, such as this humpback whale, swim in the icy polar waters. They leap in the air and fall back into the water with a splash. This is called breaching.

streamlined—having a smooth body shape that moves easily through the water

Changing coats

Harp seals are born with fluffy white coats. The mothers take care of their babies for around two weeks, and then the pups grow gray adult coats and must care for themselves.

Tusk tools

Walrus drag themselves out of the water, using their tusks as levers. They also use their tusks to remove shellfish from the seabed.

tusks—long teeth that poke out of an animal's mouth

albatross

Flying squad

Many seabirds spend the summer at the poles. Most live on land, flying out over the sea and diving to catch food. The albatross stays at sea for most of the time, only coming ashore to lay its eggs.

Pointy eggs

Guillemots lay their eggs on cliff ledges. The eggs are pointed at one end. If the eggs are nudged, they spin in a circle and do not fall off the cliff.

seabird—a bird that lives near the sea and feeds from the sea

Cliff colonies

Puffins make their nests high up on cliffs so that predators cannot reach them. They breed in large, noisy groups called colonies.

breed—to produce babies

Crowds of penguins

Penguins live in the coastal areas of the Antarctic. These birds cannot fly, but they use their wings to glide underwater as they chase their food.

Group hug

These young emperor penguins are huddling together to stay warm. They take turns to go in the middle, where it is warmest.

glide—to move smoothly through the water

Sliding along

To travel quickly on land, Adélie penguins slide over the snow on their bellies. They use their wings to push and steer.

Feet off the ground

The ice is much too cold for young chicks. To stay away from it, they stand on their mom's or dad's feet and snuggle under a special flap of skin on the adult's belly.

steer—to move in the right direction

Inuit people

The Inuit people live in North America and Greenland. Traditionally, they traveled in family groups and survived by fishing and hunting. Today many Inuit live in towns.

Cozy icebox

When they are on hunting trips, Inuit people build igloos as temporary homes. Although they are made from frozen blocks of ice and loose snow, igloos are cozy and warm inside.

temporary—lasting for a short time

Boat sense

The Inuit are expert boatbuilders. They cover their boats in sealskin, which keeps them watertight. This boat is an umiak.

watertight—*something that keeps out water*

A herder's life

Some Sami, Lapp, and Chukchi people are herders. They follow wild reindeer herds and settle in camps wherever the reindeer stop to feed.

Reindeer power

Reindeer pull sleds and carry heavy loads and riders. They also provide meat to eat and skins for clothing and shelter.

herders—people who care for herds of animals

Winter warmth

These men are wearing warm winter coats, called parkas, made from reindeer skin. The soft, warm fur is worn against the men's skin.

Mobile homes

Arctic herders move several times each year, so their homes have to be simple and lightweight. They live in tents made from cone-shaped wooden frames covered with reindeer skins.

lightweight—designed to weigh as little as possible

Polar exploration

Many explorers risked their lives trying to be the first people to set foot on the poles. In 1909 Robert Peary reached the North Pole. In 1911 Roald Amundsen beat Robert Scott in a race to the South Pole.

Modern-day explorers

Today's polar explorers wear layers of specially designed clothing to stay warm in freezing temperatures. They pull their supplies on lightweight sleds.

An explorer's best friends

Amundsen and his team learned from Arctic peoples and used husky dogs to pull their sleds. Huskies are strong and intelligent and are well adapted to the cold.

Over sea and land

Scott and Amundsen sailed part of the way to the South Pole. Once they reached land, they loaded their supplies onto sleds and continued their journeys on skis.

Scott's ship, the **Terra Nova***'*

Modern life

Improvements in transportation, food, construction, and clothing have brought a modern way of life to the Arctic. Most people now live in small towns and work in modern industries.

Arctic towns

Arctic towns are like other small towns, except that water has to be delivered by trucks. The water would freeze if it was distributed through pipes.

People carriers

The people living in polar lands no longer rely on animals for transportation. Today they travel on snowmobiles— motorized sleds.

industries—businesses that make goods and sell these goods for money

Oil industry

The Arctic's rich supplies of oil are processed in factories like this one. Oil is one of the world's most important fuels and is used to make many products. The oil industry provides jobs but harms the Arctic environment.

environment—*the natural surroundings*

Scientific research

The only people who live in Antarctica are scientists working in research stations. They study Antarctica's wildlife and find out about its climate.

Weather watching

Every day scientists measure and record the weather conditions. These measuring instruments are attached to a balloon that floats 12 miles above ground.

climate—*the usual weather conditions in one place over a period of time*

Drilling for information

Using a special drill, scientists extract long samples of ice—called cores. These layers of ice have built up over thousands of years. Studying them helps scientists learn about Earth's past climate.

Animal tracking

A tag on this Weddell seal's tail helps scientists record when and where they see this particular seal. This helps us learn more about seals' lives and how to protect them.

extract—to dig out carefully

Protecting wildlife

People have lived in the Arctic for thousands of years without harming the environment. Recently, however, people have endangered wildlife by hunting and pollution.

Free ride home

Polar bears are rare, and most northern countries have laws to protect them. Bears that wander into towns are caught and airlifted back to the wild.

pollution—*chemicals and other materials that damage the environment*

Watching and protecting

These tourists in Antarctica are on a carefully organized trip. This helps make sure that the wildlife is not disturbed very much.

Saving sea mammals

Special sanctuaries in the Southern Ocean protect the feeding grounds of whales and orcas. Most countries have agreed not to hunt in these areas.

orca (killer whale)

sanctuaries—safe places that are protected from damage by humans

Super snowflakes

Make a paper snowflake

Real snowflakes have six sides (or points), so you need to fold a piece of paper into six sections before you can create a pattern.

Place the plate onto the piece of white paper. Using a pencil, trace around the plate to make a circle. Then cut out the circle shape.

You will need
- Plate
- White paper
- Pencil
- Scissors
- Construction paper (optional)
- Glue (optional)
- Glitter (optional)
- Shiny paper (optional)

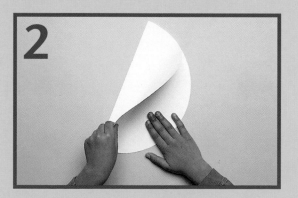

Use the white paper circle you have made to create your snowflake. Start by folding the circle in half to make a semicircle.

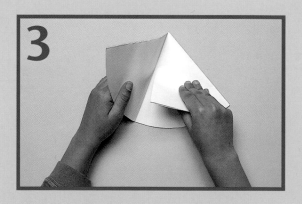

Fold the semicircle into three equal parts, as shown, to make six sections. This means that your snowflake will have six sides.

4

5

Draw a pattern on your folded paper. Make sure that you do not draw completely across the paper. You could start by copying this pattern.

Cut away sections of the folded paper, following the pattern. Be careful not to cut completely across the width of the paper.

6

Have fun making and displaying lots of snowflakes. You can glue your snowflakes onto colored construction paper and decorate them with glitter and shiny paper.

Unfold your snowflake carefully. You will see that the patterns on each of the six sections are identical—just like a real snowflake!

Ice fun!

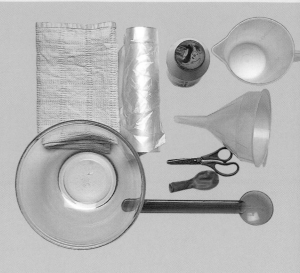

Incredible iceberg
An iceberg may take thousands of years to form from layers and layers of snow. You can make your own iceberg overnight.

You will need
- Pitcher
- Water
- Balloon
- Funnel
- Plastic bag
- Freezer
- Clear bowl
- Tablespoon
- Salt
- Scissors
- Dish towel or cloth

1 Fill the pitcher with cold water. Put the funnel into the neck of the balloon and hold it in place. Ask an adult to help you fill the balloon with the water.

2 Ask an adult to tie the end of the balloon in order to seal the water inside. Put the balloon inside a plastic bag and place the bag in a freezer overnight.

3 The next day fill the clear bowl three fourths full with water. Then add around five to ten tablespoons of salt to make saltwater.

4 Take the balloon out of the freezer and remove the plastic bag. Cut the end off the balloon and carefully peel it away from the ice.

5 Using a dish towel or cloth so that your fingers do not stick to the cold ice, carefully place your iceberg in the bowl of salty water.

Your iceberg will float in the salty water. You will see that only a small portion of the whole iceberg stays above the water's surface.

Penguin game
Play the penguin game and pretend to be a penguin keeping its egg safely above the cold ice.

You will need
- Beanbag

Penguins keep their eggs and babies safely above the ice by carrying them on their feet. To play the penguin game, you and a friend need to pass a beanbag "egg" to each other without dropping it on the floor, using only your feet.

Penguin mask

Make a penguin face

Rockhoppers are small Antarctic penguins with brightly colored faces. Make a penguin mask, and you can look like one!

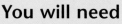

1 Start by tracing the rockhopper penguin template at the back of this book. Then transfer your tracing onto your piece of black construction paper.

You will need
- Tracing paper
- Pencil
- Black construction paper
- Scissors
- Modeling clay
- Apron
- Red and yellow paint
- Elastic
- Glue
- Yellow tissue paper

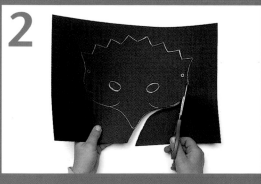

2 Using the scissors, carefully cut out the shape of the penguin mask. You may want to ask an adult to help you do this.

3 Use a pencil and modeling clay to pierce holes for the elastic strap and for the eyeholes. Enlarge the eyeholes using scissors.

4

5

Wearing an apron, paint your penguin mask. Use red for the eyes and orange for the beak. (Make orange paint by mixing red paint and yellow paint.)

When the paint is dry, cut a piece of elastic that is long enough to fit around your head. Tie the ends into each of the small holes on the sides of the mask.

6

Cut a few strips of yellow tissue paper. Spread a thin line of glue above the eyes and glue on the strips of tissue paper to make the penguin's feathery eyebrows.

Have fun wearing your mask and pretending to be a rockhopper penguin!

Index

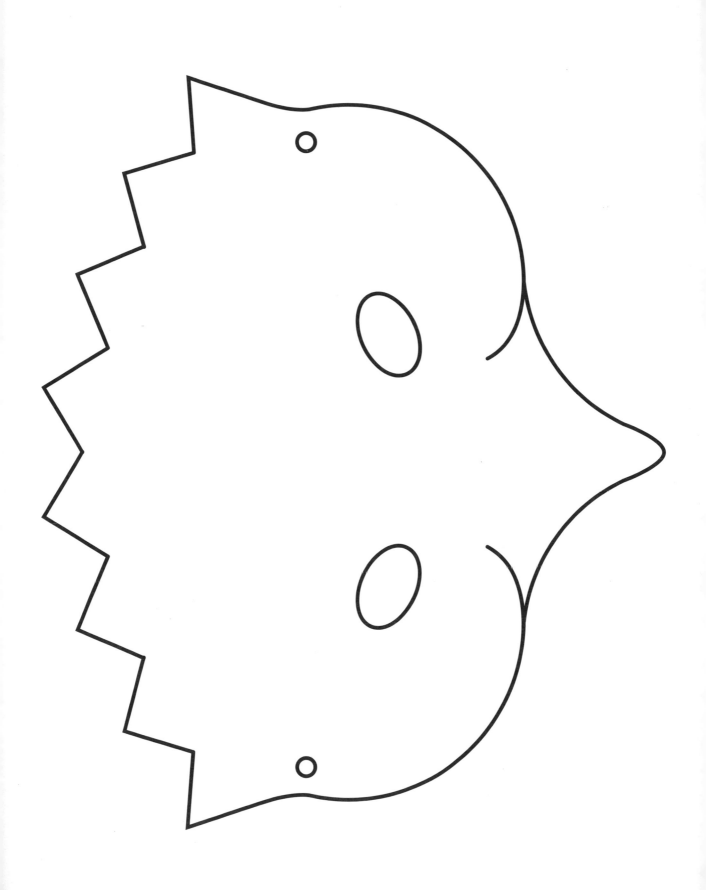